"*The Ten Secrets* is a true pleasure to read. It captures the reader's heart with delightful stories that provide gentle reminders of how to live a simple yet fulfilling life."

Nydia Han, Television Reporter

\*\*\*

"...using both Siddhartha-like wisdom and homespun advice that is vintage Forrest Gump... Edwards has accomplished his goal of fulfilling his belief in 'getting medicine in your candy...' this is, after all, a man who has come to find happiness in the everyday by simply appreciating that which is already there."

Erin Haley, Times Philadelphia

\*\*\*

"This book holds very simple yet powerful messages that can only be found in our innermost being."

Margaret M. Preston, DCSW, LCSW
Psychotherapist

# the ten
# secrets

## a father's last gift

## .there's always a second chance

## Scott Michael Edwards

sMe
Philaelphia, Pa

First sMe Edition 2005

For more information go to
www.thetensecrets.com

Manufactured in the United States of America.

Special thanks for the editing help of Mike and
Bridget Libert of Main Line Print Shop and Meg
and Pat Christensen.

ISBN 0-9777021-0-3

This book is dedicated to my family and friends. It is my hope that each of you will see a piece of yourselves in this story and understand that without you, there would be no secrets to reveal. Thanks to all of you for your support.

- Scott

# Contents

# The Prologue

I stare at my reflection.

It stares back, cool and hard, as if sizing me up for a fight.

My eyes are sharp, but dead. No life.

Deep circles betray a sleepless night.

A jolt courses through my body shifting my attention.

I re-fix my gaze and see a pair of now unfamiliar eyes: open, vulnerable and sad.

A short, deep wave of sorrow runs across my face.

Get it together, Christian, I admonish.

I run my hand through my hair and shake it off.

I'm finally out the door and on the way to my why-the-hell-am-I-doing-this job.

Money, that's why. Oh yeah. Gotta have it.

In fact, if I don't have more than anyone else I know I'll be a failure. That's the measuring stick for my life.

It's my daily routine: I get up and navigate the human habitrail of Manhattan and the labyrinth of Wall Street to find the cheese.

Yeah, it's a rat race.

That's why it pays to be king rat.

Along the way I pass the fruit vendor selling peaches, blueberries and prunes. What a poor slob, I think. He'll never have anything.

Seeing his woeful existence somehow fills mine with meaning.

This is my life. I feel sorry for you.

Don't look at my Prada shoes, Panerai watch, custom suit (you buy off the rack?), Hermes tie or

Gucci sunglasses. Just take in the smug look on
my face. Closer. Come on, closer. It tells you all
you need to know.

People ask me if I'm happy. Am I happy?

Who has time to think of that? I've got direction, a
goal, and I'm going to get there.

I've never been worried too much about happiness,
that albatross that keeps weak people from getting
ahead.

No mushy "I love yous." No whining. No time for
trite exchanges of vapid pleasantries.

Happy is something people with nothing to do
worry about.

I turn the corner and hear the strained sounds of
an accordion. A crowd has gathered blocking the
sidewalk. Annoying.

There on the curb, an older Eastern European
looking man rhythmically squeezes the worn
instrument. He clangs one bad note for every ten.
At his feet lies an open accordion case. He actually
expects to get paid for this noise?

It's like living in a carnival, I think to myself as I
begin to push by.

Out of the corner of my eye I catch his head swaying in tune, but his eyes wander off, detached. I look next to him and see a cane, the type often used by the blind, propped against a light pole. I look back at his eyes. They're not looking anywhere, just floating.

I'm slightly stunned by the insensitivity of my thoughts. Harsh, even for me.

I decide to stop and listen in a moment of penance and tribute, as his music strikes a beautiful, melancholy chord. I note that he carries himself with a sense of dignity. His suit jacket probably looked damn good twenty years ago and that about sums up the rest of him. I'll bet those bad notes would be far fewer in between with a new accordion.

"Excuse me, buddy." A hurried commuter presses past. I let him go.

My eyes spy a bank clock. Oh, crap.

What was I thinking?

I hail a taxi and, after a harried ride, arrive at work.

Banks of television monitors barking out the latest morning financial news from CNBC and Bloomberg line the walls of the trading room.

Perched above, a giant ticker announces an endless stream of prices.

The screens and tickers ring an open pit the size of a basketball court, brimming with rows of traders beginning their morning work.

Numbers dancing in their eyes, they work phones attached to their heads, calling out numbers, soothing egos, trading Cheshire grins and cussing into the air.

The buzz of the trading room never ceases to excite me, the perfect stimulant for an adrenaline junkie.

I pull into my office, take a seat and check the currency positions from the night before.

I just made more money in one night than most of you will make all next year.

More smug satisfaction. Can you feel it? Sure you can.

The message light on the phone blinks. What!?

Beep. "Chris, my name is Carl Parker. I'm an attorney for your father. Please give me a call at your earliest convenience."

Now, a phone call like this would set off warning signals for most people.

And they would for me as well except for two things: One, I haven't seen my father in fifteen years; and two, that's because he died fifteen years ago.

Still, it's impossible not to be curious.

I call Carl with practiced skepticism.

"Carl, Christian Mathews returning your phone call."

"Chris, I'm sorry to inform you, but your father has passed away."

I quash the wellspring of sarcasm boiling up inside me.

Well, almost.

"Carl, my good man, I very much appreciate the notice, but you're fifteen years too late."

Says Carl, not without some caring in his voice, "Chris, that was your adopted father, this was your real father."

Now, there's not much in this world that can shock me...

"Excuse me?"

"Perhaps you should come by my office."

"Carl, I don't have time to play CSI. What the hell are you talking about?"

"Chris, you were adopted right after you were born. Your real father just passed. I'm sorry."

The slow realization that there's some reality in this conversation sinks in. Questions flood my suddenly taxed brain.

The trading floor, so tangible to me on a normal day, now looks far removed, familiar faces reduced to caricatures.

Two fathers?

It can't be, can it?

My mind whirs. "Chris?"

"Chris, are you there?"

"Yeah, I'm here."

"I know this is a shock to you, but there's no easy way to break these things."

My mind rallies back.

Who the hell is Carl? What is the context of this phone call? I go on the offensive.

"I'm sorry, Carl, could you please give me some background on yourself and how you claim to know a claimed father?"

Suffice it to say, he proved himself in short order.

It was true. I had two fathers.

My orderly world had been reordered forever.

§

# The Funeral

It was a lavish funeral somewhere in the middle of
nowhere Pennsylvania where my father of
unknown origin made his existence.

The funeral was a who's who of who the heck? It
appeared my natural father befriended every sort of
person who ever walked, or crawled, the face of the
earth.

It was a people collection that would make Andy
Warhol smile.

Some traits just don't make the trip down genetic
lane.

I learned through brief discussions, none of which
were initiated by me, that my natural father,

heretofore referred to as my 'real' father, was a gypsy of sorts.

He didn't seem to have much purpose in life other than to gather people. He collected them like trading cards, focusing on the eclectic or discarded. People I normally wouldn't bother to sneer at, most people wouldn't.

I never discerned a profession, but he seemingly made money for himself somehow. Okay, seemingly a lot of money.

The eulogy was remarkable for what it wasn't. It wasn't about accomplishments. It wasn't about the impact he had on society. It wasn't about his legacy.

It was about the love he had for other people. An intense love for the forgotten and misbegotten; souls who will never know great success or fame, yet have found riches.

Would it not have been so politically unpalatable I would have asked for a blood test on the spot.

Then there were the pictures of my father; they were downright eerie.

There was no mistaking the jutting jaw line or the slightly crooked nose, in these we were twins, twenty years removed. But his eyes were different.

They sparkled. They danced with life. There was magic in them where I had none.

Clearly, my real father was hooked on a drug of some sort.

§

# The Quest

Back in his office, Carl looks at me with an intense stare that makes me feel far less than my age. I'm not sure how I started off in a position of submission to him, but here I am, not unlike a convicted felon awaiting sentencing.

There is something angelic about Carl. Now that I think about it, there was something angelic about everyone at my real father's funeral. I don't mean halo over the head angelic, it just seemed like they were all in on some great joke that I wasn't.

I'm used to being the smartest person in the room, but there I felt like an outsider with nothing to say. Everyone else seemed connected to something I didn't understand.

"Your father has left you a substantial fortune," says Carl, but his tone told me there is more to this.

"Really?" I remark. Asking him, without asking, to explain the catch. There certainly is one.

"The fortune will be yours at the end of your journey, should you choose to take it," Carl continues.

This is usually the point where I cut through the small talk and try to get to the point, but something in Carl's demeanor makes me patient. Strange.

"My journey?"

"Your father has asked that you meet with ten people whom he feels have a message, something to say about life, something important."

My manipulation sensor goes off. 'Something' doesn't sound right.

"And if I don't want to meet with these ten people?"

"You will forfeit a substantial fortune. A fortune that dwarfs your current bank account by an order of magnitude."

My BS detector rises to def-con one. "By an order of magnitude? Define order of magnitude in dollars and cents," I demand.

"Chris, just by knowing this small amount about your father you should know better than to ask such a question. Dollars meant nothing to this man, yet they flocked to him like moths to a flame.

"I will add this one point. If you meet with these ten people and can prove you understand their messages, by the time you are done, you too will have the keys to unthinkable wealth."

For a guy who makes damn good coin already, this deal sounds suspect. It has all the hallmarks of a setup — I can smell it.

But for reasons beyond dollars and cents, beyond rational thought and in spite of the alarm bells ringing in my head, I feel compelled to take on this task. Perhaps it is curiosity, perhaps it is my unacknowledged longing for something else in life, but he has me hooked and I am not happy.

My patience runs thin. "Give me the list of ten people and I'll meet with them." My tone means no is not an option, yet no is about to come.

"Chris, it doesn't work that way. According to your father's orders, you are to meet with these people one at a time. After you meet with each person, you are to correctly relate to me their lesson, their secret. Only after you do that for one name, do you get the next."

Carl doesn't get it.

"Well, that's idiotic. I don't have the time, and frankly, I don't want to meet with these people. I suggest you and I make a deal right here, right now, and save us both a lot of time and wasted energy."

My eyes bore into him.

I expect to hit a nerve, instead... I hit an artery.

Carl looks at me, and I swear to God he looks at me with the eyes of the father I never knew.

He gushes love. Gushes.

It pours out of his eyes.

His lips tremble.

His face crinkles in a way that seems to warm the entire room.

This from a lawyer, I remind you.

If I weren't so secure about my position in life, I would think his look is tinged with pity. I feel that my real father is looking at me, which is of course more than a little odd since I've never met him.

"It is your father's last wish to give you these gifts. He was a man of great wealth, great humility and great love. You will honor his life and yours by accepting this challenge."

Talk about getting put in a tough spot.

A deep breath.

Half of me wants to run, the other half to stay, the other half to scream expletives. I know, it doesn't add up, but neither does any of this.

I have no choice. I mean I do, but not really.

"When do I have to meet with these ten people?"

"Here is the first name." He pushes an envelope toward me.

"When the time is right and the secret discovered, call me, and I'll give you the next name on the list.

"Oh, one more thing, you have to see the final person four weeks to this day... or you get nothing."

§

# Secret One

## The Barber

I open the envelope.

*Bill Buxhaven*
*71 Fairmount Lane*
*(North) Philadelphia, PA*

I look at the map.  North Philadelphia.

Some would say the middle of hell.  The only reason I even know about North Philly is because of some drug or gun bust that makes national news.

I turn off the highway and descend into the slums. My black BMW oddly fits in because it doesn't. Everyone seems to give it a wide berth and an almost knowing stare.

I'll admit that part of my nervousness stems from the fact that I've lived in a mostly white world and it is quite obvious that I am leaving that world.

The further I descend into this the area, the more I feel as if I'm making a giant mistake, but not going would seem to have just as much risk.

I turn down Fairmount Lane, not exactly certain what to expect, when I see it: The twirling signature of an old fashioned barbershop.

## the ten secrets: a father's last gift

I pull closer and see that Bill's Barbershop is not like the rest of the block, nothing like it.

Whereas the other homes and businesses look to be one not-crooked inspector away from being condemned, Bill's Barbershop positively gleams, like it was built just yesterday.

I decide to follow the lead of the collection of junkers used for transportation in this area and park right in the middle of the street, the de facto business parking area in a section of the city that seems to play by its own rules.

I get out of the car and shoot an evil stare in every direction to ward off would-be criminals. I'm thinking that I must look like FBI, because everyone seems to disappear.

I walk toward the window. Oddly, the sidewalk changes right where Bill's shop begins. The cracked, weed-ridden sidewalk on either side of his domain surrounds what looks to be freshly poured concrete.

I look through the window; the place is packed. Packed.

I open the door looking back at my car.

"Oh, it's safe. Don't you worry; it's safe."

And that's how I met Bill.

Bigger than life with giant eyes that look like they are about to jump out of his head. His full lips part when he smiles revealing a keyboard of teeth that seems to have no beginning or end.

Bill is what my friends call country big. He probably never lifted a weight in his life, but you could hit him with a sledgehammer and only dent the sledgehammer.

"Have a seat. There's iced tea on the counter."

So, I sit.

I scan the walls. Pictures line the shop telling the story of a life well lived.

Pictures of family and friends and then, wait a second, something curious... a diploma?

'Bill' is Bill Buxhaven, M.D. Dr. Buxhaven!

"Mister, it's your turn," says Bill in a deep commanding tone.

"Uh, no it's not. There are all of these people in front of me."

"Ah, yes, they're in no hurry. You, on the other hand, look like you have somewhere to be."

"Are you sure?"

"Time waits for no man," he points at the chair.
And with that I take a seat.

"Just a trim."

"Sure thing."

I point to a picture of Bill with a beautiful full
figured woman. "Is that your wife?"

"Ah, she is, but she passed away some time ago."

"I'm sorry."

"Don't be, I was lucky to have had her for as long as
I did. Very lucky."

"How come you're not practicing medicine
anymore?"

Bill draws a deep breath as a smile breaks across
his face; a wave of wisdom about to wash up on my
life.

"My practice was very successful. I helped a lot of
lives, but it made no money. Most of my patients
didn't carry insurance or bank accounts. This area
is... let's just say, challenged. After one particularly
bad case, a patient sued me. He won and my

malpractice insurance soared. I was losing money and couldn't afford to stay open. So now I cut hair, but I like to think I shape more than hair."

"I'm sorry," I repeat, wishing I hadn't as I glance around the room at a group of downtrodden souls. Most of them don't look like they need haircuts.

His eyes gleam.

"Don't be. I was lucky enough to get an education and meet some fantastic people in life, more than a kid from the slums could ever hope for. I am very lucky."

I can't stop myself. "But don't you ever think about what could have been?"

"I have no reason to, my life is full. I can see where someone sitting in your seat might wonder about my life, but I don't. I learned a long time ago that life is whatever you think it to be."

"Well, that sounds good in theory," I challenge, "but you spent years learning a profession, you obviously loved your wife... and you lost both. Most people would think that was horrible luck. It HAS to get you down sometimes."

Again, if I could take the words back, I would, but...

"Of course I feel those moods, but I don't let them affect how I see my life. Your perception of life can be influenced by your emotions, but your emotions are not you. You can choose happiness regardless of your moods. You can control the impulses of negativity and pessimism by using enthusiasm. Enthusiasm gives you the power to create happiness in any circumstance. I love life and therefore it loves me back."

I am mesmerized by his words and his tone. I never considered my moods were at my command. I thought they were like a bad case of the flu that you just got over at some point.

"Do you see that barber pole?" He points.

"Of course."

"Does it appear to be moving from the bottom up or left to right?"

I study the pole. "Is this a trick question?"

"Yes and no. The trick is that there is no trick. It's called the barber pole illusion. Whether the pole scrolls from left to right or bottom to top, it always appears to be going up. One can't tell just by looking at the pole which way it's actually moving underneath.

"Life is like that. All of this is an illusion and we can control how we see it. This is how I live. Regardless of which way life moves me beneath me, I continually see myself rising to the top."

"How does it look?"

He holds up a mirror. I study my reflection. "It looks great," and I mean it.

"Thank you sir, your satisfaction brings me much happiness."

"How much do I owe you?"

"Your debt has been paid many times over. Thank you for coming."

"I insist." He cuts me off. "No, I insist." His firm grasp freezes my body.

His big eyes swallow mine.

"You are a positive loving person who is capable of happiness on your own terms. Decide what those terms are and live them today."

"Uh, thank you, Bill." I feel as if I owe him for more than the haircut.

I begin toward the door and stop dead in my tracks.

My father's smiling face looks down on me from
his framed seat in Bill's barber chair over the door.

§

Back in Carl's office, he stares at me for an uncomfortable period.

"What did you think of Bill?"

"Well, I think he is a very unique man. He's lost so much in his life. To me he appears unlucky, but to him he's the luckiest man alive. To him happiness is perception."

He's doing it again. That smiling, gushing thing.

"What!?"

Without a word Carl slides an envelope across the desk with a note. I read the note.

---

### Happiness is Perception

Life is how you see it. Ideas of success and accomplishment can change with time, geography, thought and the wind. Therefore, you must control your thoughts and your perceptions, because they will ultimately determine your reality and your happiness. If you can't change your reality, change your perception of it.
- Love 'till time ends, Dad

---

# Secret Two
## The Blueberry Farmer

I open the envelope.

*Jesse Butler*
*1 Crest Drive*
*West Millington, NJ*

West Millington? Never heard of it.

Now I understand why. It's not on the map. Not on any map.

There is however a Millington, New Jersey. After a moment of thought, I decide to start there.

The drive deep into New Jersey is eye opening.

Rolling hills. A meandering river. Miles of trees. Miles and miles of them.

I turn down a gravel road. A boy is walking his dog off the leash. The dog looks happier than I can really imagine.

"Where is West Millington?"

"Mister, West Millington is that way, over that hill."

A few moments later I crest the hill and see the sign: "Welcome to West Millington."

Not a hundred feet later I see another sign:
"Leaving West Millington"

I hit the brakes, put the car into reverse and retrace
my tracks.

Almost completely hidden under a canopy of
bushes and trees is a dirt driveway that disappears
into the distance. On a tree hangs a small wooden
sign reading: "1 Crest Drive."

After a few turns down the driveway, I come upon
a small farm.

Two chocolate Labradors run up to greet me. I feel
as if I've fallen onto the set of a strange movie.

A small farmhouse near a barn sits at the end of the
driveway.

The door opens and out walks this beautiful
woman. Not model beautiful, just attractive in a
way words will never capture. She just looked so
at peace, happy... vibrant.

"Hello," she says in a quiet voice.

"Hi!"

"Shhh, the kids are napping," she hushes.

"Are you Jesse?" I had assumed Jesse was a male.

"Yes, it's nice to meet you."

I'm struck by her presence and lose myself for a second.

She pauses and waits.

"And your name is?"

"Oh, uh, Christian Mathews."

"Are you interested in the cultivated blueberries or wild blueberries?"

"Uh," damn she's pretty. "Both!" I white lie.

"Great, come this way." She starts to walk me toward the barn.

It suddenly hits me. Jesse is Jessica. Jessica Butler, a child actress from my youth. Before I can swallow the impulse...

"Aren't you... ?"

"Yes, I am."

"Wow, you were, uh, ARE great. I mean, what happened?"

She smiles and pauses long enough for me to
consider my own uneasiness.

"Nothing happened, well, nothing bad. I just
discovered my real priorities.

"I had a lot of things in life, a lot of things that
sounded good to other people, but I just wasn't
happy. I was chasing what I thought I wanted.

"After I got into my twenties, I realized every time I
got what I thought I wanted, I wanted something
else. Met a guy, a fruit vendor of all things, and
realized I was competing for something that I
already had."

She pauses and smiles with a heart stopping
twinkle.

"Turned out that vendor owned a blueberry farm."

An awkward pause.

"Let me show you the wild blueberries. They're
full of antioxidants, you know. The latest studies
show they have more antioxidant benefit than
garlic, spinach...," she makes a child-like 'smelly
face,' "...even broccoli."

I could not be more interested in something I was
completely uninterested in.

We turn down a row of blueberry bushes.

"Anyway, I was saying... I had this idea of what would make me happy: stardom, fame, money. Then I got them and I was like: Where's the rest? You know? Everyone else, who had so much less, seemed to have so much more. Sometimes less really is more, because what we think of as less is the important stuff."

I have to interrupt. "Isn't not wanting to have more a symptom of not caring, of laziness?"

"I thought so too," she added, "but then I learned that most of us haven't discovered our true desires. We end up chasing 'perceived desires,' which are rarely our real desires. Most people I know spend their time chasing things that directly conflict with their real inner desires. Doesn't matter how fast you're going if you're headed in the wrong direction."

I frown. "That doesn't add up. If it weren't for having people to compare myself to, I wouldn't be where I am today."

"And where is that?" She stares straight into my eyes.

I get tongue-tied.

She laughs and continues.

"Desire and comparison can motivate you to action, but they can also trap you in the cycle of never having enough. It's a mindset that causes chronic unhappiness. Desires can become mirages that send us on empty journeys for more things, more status and more money. No one would be any happier if every wish came true. More is not better, greener grass often looks brown up close and when you get others' things, you also get their problems."

"But what about getting ahead and getting the good things in life?"

"I already have them," she adds as if it were a rhetorical question.

"I used to think happiness was so complicated and that I needed so many things to be happy, but I found out it was simple. It's like that line from the movie, 'oh, Jerry, don't let's ask for the moon, we have the stars.' All of us already have the stars; we're just too busy chasing the moon to notice."

She flips her hair back.

"You didn't come for the blueberries, did you?"

If there is such a thing as magic, it is happening right now, right here. Well, at least for me.

"No, but I'd like some just the same."

That makes her smile. "You're lucky. You know, we usually shoot trespassers," she nods over to a shotgun nearby.

"Don't worry, I sized you up quick."

I smile nervously. "Why isn't West Millington on the map?"

"Funny thing about that," she continues as she wraps pints of berries.

"When the lines were drawn up around here, there was an old blueberry farmer. Didn't want to be in the town, in any town. He wanted to keep the simple life he had and he fought like hell for what he wanted.

"Finally, the state just decided it wasn't worth it; it was easier just to leave him be. He incorporated and created the town that's not a town.

"I gave you a couple of pints of each." She puts up her hand as I reach for my wallet.

Then, with a parting smile that could have parted my heart had I let it, she left me with this advice:

"Understand the feelings you need to be happy and know that there are many different and simple paths to achieve those feelings."

The dogs watch, both happy and simple.

I somehow wish I wasn't leaving.

§

"A lot better looking than that barber, eh?" Carl asks with a mischievous grin.

"That's an understatement."

"Beautiful, but wise," he prompts. "What did you think?"

"For her, happiness is simple."

"You sound skeptical?"

"I am skeptical."

Without a word Carl slides an envelope across the desk with a note. I read the note.

---

### Happiness is Simple

Happiness comes from an internal sense of worth. It is our natural state of being. We don't need very much to be happy, but emotions such as want and envy can sabotage our happiness by making us feel as if we do. - Love 'till time ends, Dad

---

# Secret Three
## The Coach

I open the envelope.

*"Fightin'" Jimmy McGowan*
*Elder High School*
*Cincinnati, Ohio*

Cincinnati, Ohio?

I begin to think my real father has a slightly
sadistic sense of humor.

But there's something real about 'the natti,' an
immediate deflation of hype and pretense. More
like a town stuck in adolescence on its way to city-
hood. There's a common braid of strength and
commitment running through the people here.

People I would usually call boring, I learn have a
certain nobility of pride in a city whose greatest
claim to fame other than the Reds (don't ever ask
about Pete Rose here unless you have an hour) is
chili and its offspring, what the locals call Three
Ways and Coneys.

On the outskirts of town sits Elder High School
dominating all around it. The soaring brick facade
could pass as part of an Ivy League campus. It's
easy to picture the decades of crew cuts, mop tops,
plaid skirts and turned up and buttoned down
collars that have passed through its doors.

A young girl walks by, adorable except for that spike in her nose. I can't help thinking that thing must leak.

"I'm looking for Fightin' Jimmy McGowan," I say somewhat embarrassed to refer to any adult as fightin'.

"He's coaching practice," says the girl revealing yet another spike, this one in her tongue.

I smirk with disapproval. She couldn't care less.

Dust shoots up in the distance. I hear the smack of pads and the grunt of players.

I breathe in. There's something about the smell of a football field.

I turn a corner, come upon the field and hear a pitched, lispy voice that seems to emanate from everywhere. On its orders legions of young men perform like the Marine Corps on parade.

All of the energy seems to be coming from one location. I look over and see nothing but big bodies huddled near the voice. More pile around and still more until the entire team is gathered around 'that voice.'

It was nasally and twangy, the type you'd immediately write off in the business world and some people might seek speech therapy for, but this had an imperative behind it, a wisdom; something that made you just want to listen.

So I walk closer. The raspy voice seems to be talking directly to me.

"No one gives you anything of value in this world, men. You have to earn it. It's about self-respect and that doesn't come from your friends, your wallet, your teachers or out of a bottle. It's something you carry within ya."

Drawn in, I crouch closer and spy an animated body deep within the mass of players, all of whom were dead silent, soaking up every syllable.

"The world doesn't owe you anything. Those who EXpect in this world have no self-REspect. You need to go out and fight for it. What you did out here on the practice field today was magnificent. You were tough. You worked hard. You played as a team. You earned my respect.

"But practice is over, the game is on and I'm not going to lie, they're better than you.

"They have more talent at every position, but they don't have more courage or heart. There will be moments of doubt tomorrow, that's when you need to reach down, believe in yourself and turn doubt into victory. If you believe, you will not lose... look at me... you CAN'T lose. Now go home and when you come back here tomorrow I want you ready to fight."

The players roar. Tears fly as they pound their pads. 'Elder, Elder, Elder!' they scream in unison and I want to scream with them.

I want to run on the field or through a wall or over a cliff, wherever that voice tells me to go. I'm so filled with emotion that my feet are bouncing. I can hardly control myself and I never even played this damn game.

In the middle of the chaos of the moment, the players part like the Red Sea and out walks Fightin' Jimmy McGowan.

I was expecting some big Irish tough guy off of an early 1900's fishing boat, but out emerges this wisp of a man, couldn't weigh more than a buck-fifty with lead weights in his shoes. Bone skinny with a mop of golden hair framing two of the most commanding blue eyes I've ever seen.

I'm guessing he got the name because he had to fight just to get through his day. He was the poster boy for beach-sand-kicked-in-the-face-stolen- lunch-money, but he had a presence that made him seem three times his size.

If you weren't looking directly at him you would have thought him an easy mark, that a stiff wind and a shoulder slap could have folded him like a lawn chair, but one look at his eyes told you that Fightin' Jimmy McGowan was not a man to be messed with.

And he was lookin' right at me.

"My name's Jimmy," he extends a hand, drawing me in with his eyes.

I grab his hand, "Chris."

"Great to meet you Chris. Thanks for coming out. You with the paper?"

"No"

"Good, we don't need no distractions."

"Give me a hand with this, will ya?"

I look down at three full paper grocery bags.

"Sure."

I grab one and reach for another. He beats me to it.

"I'll take that. I never ask someone to do more than I'm doing."

"What's in the bags?"

"Peanut butter and jelly, my favorite."

"Looks like you're feeding the whole team?"

"Part of 'em. They're for the boy's home. Couple of my players are in there. They're tomorrow's lunches. I bring'em every day, and a few extras for their friends," he winks at his own excess.

We start walking as the players head to the locker room still filled with energy.

"Good kids, these kids, but boy is it hard to keep their heads on straight."

"I would imagine," I say worthlessly.

"Kids these days expect things to be given to them. People always whining about this or that. It's simple really. If you want happiness, you have to work for it. Happiness requires effort."

"That's interesting you say that. I was just talking with a woman who thought happiness was simple."

"Damn it, it is simple. A man can be happy with whatever he puts his mind to, but you still got to get off your butt. Happiness requires upkeep."

"Upkeep?"

"Yeah, upkeep. If you don't tend to the garden of happiness, pull the weeds and nurture the flowers, one day you will see it overgrown. There's two truths in life: One is that things are either goin' forward or backward. Two is that if you're not goin' forward you're goin' backward. That's why you've got to work at your relationships, family, spirit, you name it. If you don't, you start to lose it."

Jimmy was a walking dichotomy. One of the most powerful speakers I'd ever met in one of the most physically un-intimidating bodies I'd ever seen.

"Most of the time when people are feeling down they walk around all mopey talking about what they could have or should have done instead of just doing it. See, the world cares little what you 'thought' about doing if those thoughts are not followed by action. Intention without action diminishes self-worth and happiness. Life makes you get off your butt."

"People are busy," I say meekly, expecting to be rightly slapped.

"Hogwash, that's an excuse. There's always time. If you love your children, you must do the actions that show love. If you want more friends, you have to find and nurture friendships. It doesn't get any simpler than that, yet people are always trying to think their way around things rather than just doin' em."

We come upon a pick-up truck.

"Here ya go. Just throw it in the back here," says Jimmy.

"That's real nice of you to do this."

"Nice? Hell it's a privilege. My father always said that a man who can't find time in his day to do one good thing for another ain't a man, but a leech."

The leech speaks.

"I think a lot of times people are just afraid of failing or trying something new, so they don't do anything."

Jimmy makes a face like he ate bad food.

"We're all afraid. Every single one of us is a coward. Hell, I'm a coward, that's why I work so hard. You know I married the prettiest girl in my class? Look at me. You're probably asking yourself right now: How the hell did you get her? I'll tell ya. I asked and asked and asked again and fibbed about my dancing ability and I got the girl. If I'd let my fear take over I'd still be single. Happiness involves doing and risk. Better to have dared and failed than never to have dared at all. Dare to be happy. That's what I say."

Jimmy gets in his truck. "Thanks for the help, Chris."

"My pleasure, Jimmy. Good luck tomorrow."

"Luck comes to those who work at it, right?"

"Right."

"Well, I'm feelin' lucky."

§

"Hey Carl."

"Hey Chris, how was the trip to Cincinnati?"

"My father had a sense of humor didn't he?"

"And a sense of irony," he adds with a satisfied snort.

At this point I know the drill.

"Jimmy seems to think that happiness requires work."

Carl laughs. "Jimmy IS a piece of work."

Without a word Carl slides an envelope across the desk with a note. I read the note.

---

### Happiness Requires Work

The world does not work for those who don't work for themselves. Give up on the feeling that the world somehow owes you and gain self-respect. Entitlement is self-defeating, it only keeps you down. - Love 'till time ends, Dad

---

# Secret Four
## The Frog Keeper

I open the envelope.

*Mary Guilfoyle*
*701 Peachtree Lane*
*Santa Barbara, California*

Now we're talking. Santa Barbara is a place worth traveling for.

I drive along the beach front, top down, Springsteen playing, while along the wide path sun-lovers mix with distance runners, bikini-gazers and time killers.

The beauty of the vision imprints the moment in my mind.

But with the sun on a downward arc, I make my way into the hills.

I'm now on Peachtree Lane. A stately brick wall lines the street leading to a small gate where hangs a sign:

*701 Peachtree Lane*

The place is breathtaking.

The hedges perfectly trimmed, the flowers blooming and the air filled with their fragrance and the fresh smell of sea winds.

Two gigantic trees hold baskets of luscious looking peaches dotting the cascade of leaves like a galaxy of small red moons against the night sky.

I wouldn't be surprised to see an English prince dismounting his polo horse in the distance.

But something's amiss.

The more I take in the mansion the more I realize it's not a mansion at all, but a home of some sort.

I pan around. Grey hair topped wheel chairs crisscross walkers holding up well-lived bodies, some of whom seem to be barely holding onto life.

I ask at the front desk for Mary Guilfoyle. Mentioning my father's name brings a smile to all who hear it, which brings a smile to me.

"So nice of you to stop by. She's having a really good day."

"A good day?"

"Yes, a very good day. Yesterday wasn't her best. She's out by the frog pond right now. She'd love the company."

I walk outside, not quite feeling up to today's task.

Off in the distance I see a walker framed by two small ponds, one on top of the other, seemingly flowing into each other.  I walk closer.

Just to the left of the walker, I see a woman kneeling in a flowerbed, tending the garden.

At the edge of the frog pond sits a small cartoonish-looking frog, his oversized flippers poised for action, watching intently for flying food.

Just feet away, the woman's freckled hands work the soil with care.  Her face contorts with concentration as she sets a tulip in just the perfect position.  I pan from her body to the walker.  She's laid an almost perfect patch of multicolored tulips leading right to the frog pond.

I'm amazed by the care and frankly the skill she's used to create a river of flowers that more resembles an impressionist painting.

"They love the flowers!"

She catches me off guard with a beguiling grin that looks like it could have come from a twenty year old.

"The frogs, that is."  She points and sighs with caring.  "His name's Henry."

"He's my best friend." She turns away and begins to plant another tulip.

This strikes me at once as absurd and possibly the saddest thing I've ever heard.

Her words cut through to my heart.

Sorrow wells up deep within.

My throat constricts.

My eyes moisten.

My skin tingles.

Oh shit, I'm going to cry.

Something I haven't done since the euro tanked two years ago.

I feel guilty worrying about my own problems that really aren't.

I ponder her revelation; it distresses me beyond words.

While I take her in, the frog seems to be looking at me and her at the frog in a comical triangulation of thought and curiosity.

I can feel sadness building within me seeking an outlet, but just before the dam breaks, her eyes halt my pity and turn it back on myself.

They're not sad. In fact, her eyes are positively beaming with pride and love.

"Isn't this a beautiful moment?" She sighs.

Well, of all the things I've considered in this world to be beautiful, an old lady covered in dirt looking longingly at a big footed frog is not at the top of the list, the bottom or anywhere near the list. I'm partial to a tight bikini on a beach next to a dripping cold glass with a wedge of lime in it.

She smiles almost mischievously and I recognize that 'look' from my father's funeral.

Not her specific face, mind you, but that *look*.

*That* look.

The look like she gets the joke of life and I don't.

"There is only now. Happiness is experienced in the present moment. Can you feel the moment?"

I am suddenly filled with contradiction and confusion.

Yes, I can feel it, the moment, but for some reason I don't want to.

I have this overwhelming instinct that giving in to this moment would somehow invalidate, well, everything, my past, my life and my future life as I saw it. Everything I've done or was about to do.

This damn lady and her stupid pet frog best friend were challenging my entire belief system with one question.

"Yes," I manage to choke out of my mouth.

She smiles deeply, admiring the moment.

"If you fixate on the past or the future you will miss the happiness of the moment." She adds lightly, looking back over her work, radiating warmth and happiness.

On her last word, Henry leaps into the air and plunks into the pond underneath rippling rings that disappear into the water's edge.

"Could you help me get up?"

"Uh, sure," I mutter as if I'm the elderly one.

She takes my help only so far as she needs it, to the walker. Once there she looks at me.

"I'll drive from here."

She dusts herself off as much as she's able. I lean in to help her.

"Don't get fresh with me," she warns.

I jump back, embarrassed.

"That is, unless you plan to do something about it," she adds with a little vinegar.

I laugh. Together we walk back, slowly passing her neighbors who wave or nod and say hello, checking me out suspiciously in the process.

"Most of these people here, they're nice, but they're always looking for ways to be unhappy. They're always looking for the one thing that's wrong instead of the infinite number of things that are right."

"I guess that's human nature," I say somewhat stupidly.

"Human nature is to be happy," she contradicts. "We think our way into unhappiness.

"So many people miss so many moments, the good stuff, because they're waiting to be happy when they get something they think they want, when all they have to do is live in the moment."

"Well, some of us do want things in life. We have goals," I butt in.

"Oh, don't fall into that trap," she dismisses.

"Don't postpone happiness waiting for 'A Big Happiness,' such as marriage, money or achievement. Deferment teaches your mind the 'habit of unhappiness.

"You sound like you're waiting on the future, don't."

I feel like a scolded school kid.

But she's just getting going and picking up speed at the same time, bustling with so much energy I worry she's going vault her walker.

"Have you ever read Jane Austen?"

"Well, uh, no. I don't think so."

"No one reads anymore," she protests.

She's performing now and I'm a ready audience.

She takes one hand off her walker and waves it dramatically in the air. "How often is happiness destroyed by preparation, FOOLISH preparation." She finishes with emphasis.

"That's Jane Austen. You should read more."

"I know." I reply unconvincingly.

She's undeterred.

"Now Jack over there is the most miserable guy in the world. He's stuck in the past and waiting on a future that will never come. He thinks about what was and what went wrong with his marriage and thinks he can only be happy if he gets his ex-wife back. I mean, why would anyone want such a miserable person?"

She has a point and one look at Jack tells much. Physically, he's still a handsome man even if life has etch-a-sketched years all over his face, but his dour look erases all the good work nature has done.

"But he's going to stay miserable, because he's stubborn. If he'd learn to live in the moment and appreciate life, he actually could get her back. But he waits and waits, and he'll likely wait to be happy until he's dead.

"Don't wait to be happy, young man."

We approach the door.

"It's time for my nap now. Thank you for spending these moments with me. I'll cherish them."

Again that smile, as the door shuts behind her.

§

"She's an incredible woman," I say to Carl before he can ask.

Carl just smiles.

"She thinks that happiness is found in the moment."

"What do you think?"

"I'm not sure."

Without a word Carl slides an envelope across the desk with a note. I read the note.

---

### Happiness is in the Moment

Don't live in the past or be caught waiting on the future. Live in the ebb and flow of life's moments. Experience the joy of now by seeing the good and the beauty in your world and being grateful for what you have. - Love 'till time ends, Dad

---

# Secret Five
## The Whale Watcher

I open the envelope.

*Dan Anderson*
*A Whale of a Trip Adventures*
*Orcas Island, WA*

You might be wondering about my job about now. Well, it's no coincidence that my job is wondering about me. Extended leaves of absence are usually tickets to permanent leaves of absence in my world.

But I am sucked in, by blood and thought and wonder.

I feel something changing within me, like God, whatever God means, is rearranging my brain like a puzzle.

If I stop now, I'll be unfinished, unable to go back or go forward, stuck in a purgatory of confused thought.

While my mind spins in circles, my eyes are fixated outside the plane window, on the ghostly visage of a giant snow-capped mountain piercing a suspended sea of clouds. I look off in the distance; there's another and another.

It is heaven from above and I feel a tinge of spirituality, a connection. Maybe I am starting to

at least understand the joke, even if I don't get it all
together.

The plane banks hard and the giant thumb of
Puget Sound plunges into view.

As we descend, the mountains bloom around us,
framing the entire area with a giant backdrop so
absurdly beautiful it looks like a Hollywood set.
Surreal.

An hour later I'm in a ferry churning through Puget
Sound with the city of Seattle shrinking into the
distance.

The Pacific Northwest is the end of the earth. But
if this is the end, my beautiful friend, I'm happy.

A hyperkinetic city boy, I feel strangely at peace in
this detached part of the world.

But as the ferry ride drags on, part of me begins to
doubt. The doubting part of me feels as if I'm
being manipulated, sent on a bit of a red herring
scavenger hunt.

Then the words of Dr. Buxhaven come to me: *"You
can control the impulses of negativity and pessimism by
using enthusiasm."*

I decide to bury the negativity and focus on the enthusiasm of the moment. It works. I get excited about the journey ahead. In fact, I'm somewhat childlike.

A silly grin takes over my face, a grin of defiance or maybe triumph over self, like I just broke loose from some life-limiting gravitational pull.

The ferry docks with a giant clunk that shakes the boat from front to back and front again. The locals take it in stride. My smuggled martini flies over the rail.

I don't want to over-dramatize it, but I'm giddy, as free and inspired as the place I've just landed.

Orcas Island is famous for the orca whales that do laps around the island in search of food. Oddly it was not named for the whales, but in honor of Don Juan Vincente de Guemes Pacheco Padilla HORCASitas y Aguayo Conde de Revilla Gigedo of Spain.

Sometimes irony is ironic, no? Don't tell Alanis.

"The horseshoe-shaped island is a magical mix of lush forest, farm valleys, placid lakes and stunning mountains, all wrapped around a beautiful fjord."

That's what the tourist guide says and I'm inclined to agree. Except I have no idea what a fjord is or how to say it.

There are no rental cars here.

The best I can do is a scooter.

I look like a dork on this thing puttering along in my helmet emblazoned with "Rental" on the back of it. But with no one I know around to see me, I'm actually kind of digging it.

I wonder how many other little things might seem more fun if no one was judging or looking. Or maybe if I just didn't care.

In the middle of the little town that dots the top of the fjord (a long, narrow, deep inlet of the sea), around which the rest of the island appears to melt, is 'A Whale of a Trip Adventures.'

There, I say hello to Dan Anderson.

Dan is my height and somewhere about my age, but harder looking.

His shaved head and wry smile give him the look of a modern day pirate, but he has open eyes that hint at a softer soul underneath.

He books passengers for the whaling boat with a casual pleasure. I watch him astutely.

I contrast his moments of satisfaction with my daily trading rituals of highs, lows, voluminous stomach acid and migraine headaches.

He just seems content. It is finally my turn.

"Can I help you, man? We're about to take off. Last trip of the day if you want in."

"Uh, yeah. Sign me up," I hand over a credit card. He looks at his watch.

"No time, this one's on me. Head out this way."

Before I know it we're loaded on to the boat, the engines roar to life and we're churning out to sea.

To our left, Mt. Constitution soars to its commanding perch, keeping a watchful eye as the sea opens up before us.

The motors die down and Dan points out a sight a New Yorker only sees in books or on The Discovery Channel after dinner reservations are canceled.

"If you look off to your right, between the two tall trees in the middle, no, THERE! To the left. You'll see a bald eagle, Swallah. He's our resident hunter and showman."

Almost on command the giant eagle takes flight, zooming over our boat headed for the far side of the fjord. He disappears into the trees. A giant bird commotion commences, and out of the trees scream two giant ravens hot on the tail of Swallah.

A pitched aerial dogfight unfolds over the boat, with the ravens driving the eagle off.

"Round one to the Ravens," exclaims Dan with satisfaction.

The engines come back to life as Swallah returns to his perch, waiting again for his next moment to strike.

Dan takes us safely out into Puget Sound and cuts the engines.

"We're right in the path of their usual food run. Some guys'll chase the pod, I like to let'em come to me."

Dan passes out beer like champagne and sightseers snap them up.

He props up next to me, taking in the view he's seeing for the first time a thousand times over.

"You've got a nice set up out here," I say obviously.

He nods his head lightly with appreciation.

"Thanks, thanks a lot.  Never in a million years did I think I'd end up here."

"Really, what did you do?"

"Investment Banker."

A shocked look.

"Wow, that's a switch."

"You're tellin' me."

"How did you get here from there?"

"Was down in San Francisco working for a firm specializing in tech.  Met a girl from Seattle, fell in love, quit my job and moved there.  I was convinced I'd found 'the one.' You know.  The only one for me."

"I could never do that," I say with admiration.

"Didn't think I could either, but I figured you only get one roll of the dice; go for it."

"I'm impressed."

He shakes that off. "Nothing stays the same, better I make the decision than fate, right? Happiness involves change, risk and growth."

"That's inspiring. Did you marry her?"

"No, she dumped me for some internet shlump I helped take public. The market tanked and I didn't have a job to go back to, so I moved up here to commune with nature.

"Greatest thing that ever happened to me. I discovered a whole different type of happiness, in touch with the land and people. Met another girl who's perfect for me. It's not really better or worse, just different."

"You were lucky."

"It's not luck, dude, it's an attitude. Those who are truly happy have an internal compass that effortlessly directs them toward positive change."

Dan cracks a beer.

"We can't become what we need to be by remaining what we are."

"That's profound."

"That's Oprah."

He shoots me a half smile.

"See, my Dad was the company guy, locked into
one way of life and when that way of life changed,
he didn't know how to handle it. He quit."

"He quit?"

"Not suicide, man. He just quit playing the game.
He thought there was only way for him to be
happy and when he lost it, job, wife, he just gave
up. I didn't want to fall into that trap, so I
followed my heart. You know those people who
say they found the only one for them?"

"Yeah, I know a lot of them."

"That's crap. That's the kind of thinking that
makes people miserable. If that person dies or
changes or moves on, you'll find another 'one.' If
you'd lived on the other side of the world you'd've
found a 'the one' there. Now it won't be the same,
better or worse, just different and that's okay.
Beware the trap of thinking there's only one
avenue for you to find happiness or one person to
find happiness with. Happiness is experienced in
many ways and has many faces."

"Well if that kind of thinking catches on, it's going
to ruin a lot of wedding speeches," I kid.

Dan grins broadly, "It'll just make'm think more about what life's really about. Fantasy world is a great place to visit, but if you try to live there you're buying into a life of disappointment. Life ain't a fairy tale. There's no Santa Claus, no Easter Bunny and the boy doesn't always get the girl, but that's alright, because the real thing is always better.

"Take the whales. We see them in the water show and they're cute and fun, but come on, dude, that's a fairy tale. Now you're going to see the real thing and it's 'sooo' much better than any staged show, because it's real."

'Whale ho,' yells some dopey tourist on cue.

We all rush to the rails as the J-pod goes by.

Their fins break the water's surface. They announce their presence with a series of yelps as they play to our delight.

If nature has created a more exquisite blend of beauty and power, I have never seen it. Giant bundles of muscle that looked painted by Disney. Conceived before man had a past, they cut through the cold blue sound water like some strange beings of the future.

I learn that each orca in the pod has a name and the locals mourn them when they die.

Dan revs up the engines and we cruise with the
pod for a half an hour. Most of the time we are
silent, watching in awe. I almost feel like calling
Mary.

A few hours later, the boat docks. My mind is
filled with visions of eagles, whales and fluorescent
starfish clinging to rock, scrawling nature's graffiti
all over the rugged cliffs. I laugh to myself,
thinking about my colleagues ending their day
bragging about their trading acumen in some bar.

I step off the boat in a dream state and this giant
hand swats me in the back.

"Now that didn't suck, did it dude?"

"That was awesome."

"That's what it's all about. I could've turned
around and headed back once I lost her, but
instead I took the gift."

A screech from above.

We turn as Swallah swoops down from the clouds
grabbing a sure hold on a tree that looks older than
time. His posture demands you look at him and
appreciate his magnificence.

Dan smiles a hidden treasure pirate smile.

"You never know what cool gift life has in store for you, but ya gotta have the courage to look at it as a gift.

"People get gifts all the time; they just mistake them for problems."

Swallah takes off on another hunt.

§

Carl looks at me now like a friend.

"Did you enjoy Orcas Island?"

"Yes, very much so. I never thought I could live like that, but after spending some time there, I could see it."

"Happiness changes, doesn't it?" Says Carl with a devilish grin.

"Apparently it does."

Without a word Carl slides an envelope across the desk with a note. I read the note.

---

### Happiness Changes

The more you embrace change and understand the magic inherent in the concept of change, the more fulfilled a life you will lead. Happiness will change because life's moments will continue to fall and build, layering our experiences and leading us in new directions. Experience the happiness of today with all of your heart, but have the courage and grace to let go and seek out and embrace the happiness of tomorrow. - Love 'till time ends, Dad

---

# Secret Six
## The Teacher

I open the envelope.

*Sangoo Han*
*7111 South Cicero*
*Chicago, Illinois*

South Cicero is not a place described with flowery words, but rather defined by grit.

Running to the southwest of downtown Chicago, it's made up of enclaves, part European ethnic, part U.S. minority.

7111 South Cicero is smack dab on a Korean street that held fast against the waves of influx and reflux.

It is also, it turns out, home to a drug rehab clinic.

This is going to be a tough one.

I park on the street and give thanks that my 7-Series is in a Manhattan garage.

No one will miss this rental if it's gone. I put the odds at 50/50 and feel better for buying the extra insurance.

As I walk toward the front door, I sense a presence walking with me, actually behind me. Like a stiff

wind, it moves me forward erasing doubt.
Somehow, I've picked up an unseen ally.

I ask at the front desk for Sangoo.

"His class is almost over. Hurry, he doesn't like
late-comers," says the woman behind the front
desk.

I walk into a crowded room, chairs lined in a U
shape. A middle-aged Korean man, Sangoo I
presume, is addressing the class. He glares at me.

"Please tell us your name," he orders.

"Christian Mathews," I reply like a kid in pre-
school at attendance.

"Please sit there," he points and orders.

I do as he asks.

I look around the room. The faces strafe me with
skepticism. I strafe right back exhibiting a
newfound confidence with the unfamiliar.

I see a slice of melting pot America held too long to
the flame. A beaten-looking multi-ethnic, multi-
gender group, trying to find a way back to society.
Whether they stayed or not was up to them, says
Sangoo.

"Your battle with meth, with crack, booze or smack is no different than any human's battle with wanton desire. It's an ancient battle complicated by modern life."

He rolls up his sleeves, revealing a horrid mess of needle tracks.

"I know this battle well. I went on a trip that wouldn't end. Got a hold of some bad stuff, really bad. Dead bad. I 'came to' in a hospital bed with a priest giving me last rites. I couldn't remember my own name, but somehow I remembered my three-month-old daughter. I'd left her at home for two days. By herself. They didn't even believe me at first, but I made them believe. We found her barely alive. She lived, but she don't live with me anymore. I had a decision to make. Get busy living or get busy dying's what they say. I was so busy dying I didn't notice I was almost dead. I buried myself in book after book after book looking for answers to overcome my addictions. I decided I had to sacrifice my addictions and commit to getting clean. And I'm as clean as I can be given what I know.

"A piece of us will always revel in the lust and like it because it feels good. But you are in control, not your lust. The body is the servant to the mind and the mind to the thought. Not the other way around.

"The key to breaking habits, any habit, is understanding your mind and cravings.

"Your body is telling you that you must have it now because it doesn't see the greater high waiting down the road.

"Now *you* have a choice to make. I have faith you will make the right one.

"Thank you for your time. Please join hands and give each other a moment of silence and courage to make the right choices."

Both of my hands are grabbed. I reflexively flinch and pull away, not wanting to grab a drug addict's hands.

But the hands tighten to the point that I can't pull back without making a scene.

I give up to the moment of silence and feel a pulse of energy travel through my body. I allow myself to join in, adding my own good wishes for these people battling serious problems.

Sangoo finishes with this thought: "Sacrifice is not about giving up, but getting rid of the shackles of indulgence to allow things of true importance into your life."

The moment of silence ends. I take my hands back, a bit ashamed of the fact that I don't want to touch another part of my body after touching these drug addict hands.

The class files out leaving only Sangoo, now sizing me up as a farmer might do to cattle at auction.

Surely this is the wisest man I've yet met. "What did you mean when you said ancient battle?"

I feel at least like a college student now and he turns from skeptic to professor.

"Our reflexive minds are programmed for a scarcity mentality. We weren't programmed for a world of abundance. At our core we still have animal instincts, to get as much as we can as soon as we can. We have so much now that our danger isn't getting enough; our danger is getting too much. Modern society is like the horse you have to stop from eating itself to death. We have to use our minds to overcome ourselves."

Well, this is an interesting theory. Humans, at the core, are out of control animals. Still, his words make sense even if I doubt his reasoning.

"We need to stop overindulging in different things that give us short-term pleasure and live with balance. We have to sacrifice one form of happiness to enjoy a greater one, in the case of many here..."

He looks me up and down as if I'm a drug addict.

"...give up the short-term high to enjoy a healthier body and mind. And in some cases we have to choose between two greater happinesses, because there's not room to experience both with quality. It's not the breadth of happiness, but the depth that brings with it meaning and personal contentment.

"People are constantly swayed by the winds of short-term gratification and make themselves regretful by focusing on what they don't have; the trick is to change your focus to what you have.

"A man sacrifices the single life to have a family. A woman may sacrifice a career. Both still may wish for their old lives even as they enjoy the family, but life doesn't have room for both at the same time. Neither is better than the other, but a commitment is required.

"Whatever you choose to do there will always be something else you had to give up to fully experience the first. That's why you have to be happy with the choices you make and want what you have, rather than focusing on having what you want.

"Once you know what you want, you have to go for it and don't look back. You can't think about what you gave up, only about what you have now. Everything worthwhile in life involves tradeoffs and sacrifice."

He smiles so deeply I feel his heart breathe.

"I have to go pick-up my little girl now. I hope you will come back. You can beat whatever it is you're addicted to. You control your mind and your thoughts, not the other way around."

"Good luck to you."

He pats me on the shoulder and is gone.

I wonder what long-term happiness I've given up by not sacrificing less important ones.

§

"We really are victims of our own success, aren't we?" I philosophize with Carl.

"Victims of our own excess," he responds.

"I think I'm beginning to understand myself a little more."

"Have you learned that happiness takes sacrifice?"

"I have now."

Without a word Carl slides an envelope across the desk with a note. I read the note.

---

### Happiness Takes Sacrifice

You can't experience every form of happiness in the world at the same time. Commit with your heart to the happiness of your choosing and do not let thought, circumstance or person prevent you from your happiness. - Love 'till time ends, Dad

---

# Secret Seven
## The Tree Whisperer

I open the envelope.

*Brownie Brown*
*Brownie's Bed and Breakfast*
*Cashiers, North Carolina*

A few hours north of the bustling suburban sprawl
of Atlanta is another world, another time, where
thousands of waterfalls are strung like Christmas
tinsel across an army of pine-smothered
mountains.

Intertwined through the giant waves of green
snakes the only road possible through this area.

An hour of driving the beautiful switchbacks is at
once breathtaking and tediously dangerous. Each
turn reveals another picture postcard and each
turn a perilous cliff.

One after the other after the other after the other.

Ascending, and then finally descending, far away
from fast food signs and giant warehouse stores
and into a world of small crafts and gentle care.

This is Brownie Brown's world.

Set back against a small lake sits her Bed and
Breakfast, full of charm, tinged with sadness and
bathed in serenity.

A family of perfectly trained German Shepherds
happily patrols the farm, easily weaving in and out
of the paths of horses.

The serenity is broken by the wail of an engine.
Up the path grinds what looks like a tricked out,
gas powered golf cart, but this one is made for hard
work.

She cuts the engine.

"Been clearing the horse trail.  Storm knocked over
a few lightweights.  Hope you weren't waiting
long," says Brownie.

Brownie doesn't have an age, not that she'll tell you
anyway, but no word is required.  She wears it on
her face and counts it with weighted words.

"No, not at all.  Just got here."

"Glad to hear it.  Welcome to Brownie's.  Here, we
hike and ride and bike and drink wine over
backgammon or chess.  Hope you like to do those
things, because there ain't much else."

"That's just fine."

She shows me to my room.  Up the stairs.  To the
right.  Second door on the left.

The key looks like it was made in the forties and I

find out that's about right.

The room couldn't be quainter, if that's a word.
Part country, part comfy. I unload my small
traveling case, put my head down and proceed to
sleep the day away.

I awaken to catch the last part of the day's sun
cutting patterns through the trees into giant
figures that morph with the minutes. Nature's
shadow play.

Out on the front deck the guests sit, eyes smiling,
enjoying a little peace and harmony and a lot of
fermentation.

I don't feel much like talking to strangers. I've
been overwhelmed by thought lately and more
than a little melancholy about my life.

A man without a figurative home. Far removed
from where I was, but not knowing where I am.

I walk around back and breathe in the air of a new
way of thinking and a new view of life. I'd like to
say everything changed in an instant and became
clear, but that would be a lie.

When everything you are, and were, is thrown off
kilter, life gets frightening.

Sometimes it seems like all the wisdom in the

world can't fight the critic, that internal voice that watches your every move, marks your every failure and knows you're a pretender. I mean, we all are to some extent.

You try so hard to keep the critic at bay, yet he always seems to be there.

I've spent my life laughing at the failures of the world, those who couldn't achieve, couldn't hack it.

I begin to realize the truth I already knew.

The reason I despise others is I despise myself. My view of the world around me is simply my view of myself.

You can't hate others and love yourself at the same time. The mind doesn't work that way.

It seems so blatantly obvious to me at this moment, that outward hate is inward hate.

Rather than find some value in this discovery, I am borderline despondent.

My inner critic is fully unleashed and now attacking mercilessly.

I wanted so much, I had so much, and I gave it away.

See, I haven't told you about the girl that I lost
some years ago, half a decade to be exact. The only
one who had my heart. The one who could see
inside mine and make the world right. When I
looked into her eyes nothing else existed.

But I didn't want her to see my heart, to give
anyone the keys to such a wretched thing, so I
turned on her and in the process turned her away.
My heart hardened more after that.

The memory of her loss reverberates discordantly
in my brain, shrouded until weakness dissolves the
anesthetic of rationalization like a mirage leaving
only emptiness; the daily lightness an unbearable
weight of nothing.

The reality made more painful because what I've
become is not who I am. I was told to be this way,
by convention, by Madison Avenue, by the rush to
have more and beat out the next guy.

By the rat race.

And I bought into it like a sucker.

Suckered by a rat.

I stare at a hanging pinecone, waiting for its time
to drop and grow. I wonder if that's me. Maybe it
just isn't my time yet.

Feeling sadness and regret, that's something right?

"The trees, they talk to you, don't they?"

Fermentation in hand, Brownie ducks under a tree branch.

"Not sure I like what they're telling me."

"Up here there's nowhere to hide, it's just you and the pines. And they tell it to you straight."

"Yeah, I guess."

"That's why they call them whispering pines. Now, some say it's because of the wind, but I know better," she looks at the trees as if they're her children.

"At least they're not yelling at you," she smiles and hands me the glass of wine with a nod. I take it and drink.

"I don't know. I'm not sure I've made such great choices."

Her lips purse in feigned disgust.

"I've lived some years and have yet to meet a perfect person. Perfection is an illusion. No one can live a perfect life. Much unhappiness is caused by having unrealistic expectations about life and making anything short of those expectations unacceptable.

"You learn to appreciate what you have."

"I just thought I knew what I wanted. Now..."

"You have to face the deep, dark truthful mirror; you can't run away from yourself."

A look of surprise.

Did she really pirate a line from Elvis Costello?

She doesn't blink. "Have you ever read Jung?"

This again? The 'no' is evident on my face and she saves mine for me. I silently vow to read more.

"He once said that all neurosis is a mere substitute for legitimate suffering."

"So, what suffering am I avoiding?"

"That's the question. Isn't it? You miss her, don't you?"

I nod.

"Things just happen. There's no way our small minds will ever fully understand the grand plan. We just have to keep pointing forward."

"Funny, that's what a friend of mine said."

She looks up at the trees as if listening to their wisdom and inhales a memory from her past.

"Resist the temptation to keep asking 'why.' You will never fully know why most bad things happen. Learn from your mistakes, but also learn to move on."

I chime in selfishly. "I just... life could have been so different."

This jogs an empathetic smile loose from Brownie's face. She's been there before.

A hint of sad beauty glints in her eyes. "You have to accept the perfect imperfection of life."

The last tentacles of sunshine withdraw into the night.

There's peace in the North Carolina sky.

I'm hoping to take some of it with me.

§

"Were my father and her ever...?"

Carl leans back in his chair, "maybe."

"I don't know why, I could just tell. I wonder what happened."

"Life doesn't always work out perfectly, does it?"

Without a word Carl slides an envelope across the desk with a note. I read the note.

---

### Happiness is Imperfect

You will never be completely happy until you accept your imperfections and the faults of those around you. Make peace and find joy amid the "perfect imperfection" of life. - Love 'till time ends, Dad

---

# Secret Eight
## The Survivor

I open the envelope.

*Denny Cippolini*
*"The Den"*
*Lincoln, Nebraska*
*(bring your workout clothes)*

Somewhere around the 90$^{th}$ meridian Mother
Nature left the iron on.

Here, the Appalachians have long given up their
fight against gravity and melted into a sea of flat.
Flying over these hectares of pancake the far
bookend of the Rockies seems like just a romantic
notion.

The only thing that separates the view out the
window of our twin-engine puddle jumper from
the end of the horizon is a distant swirling mass of
black clouds punctuated by thunderbolts
connecting heaven to earth.

Suddenly, a brilliant flash illuminates the wall of
black, fading as quickly as it struck.

"They call that that sheet lightning, because it
lights up the clouds like a sheet," says Bobby
Hogan sitting next me.

He hadn't talked since we left Minneapolis. Not a
grumble or a mumble. Just sat there, quietly,

alternating between his machinery magazine and what looks like a Nebraska football yearbook.

"I'm just glad it's over there and not here," I say somewhat nervously. I never cared for lightning or thunder, less so in a plane and in this overgrown model airplane less than most.

"Oh, I don't know about that," says Bobby with an undertone of warning. "These things can be up on you before you blink."

I turn back outside and it's like someone shifted the earth fifteen degrees. Those clouds in the distance are now barreling down on top of us, making up half the space in seemingly half a sentence.

CRACK! POP. POW!

My back wrenches as the entire sky explodes in a cascade of fireworks.

"WOO-EEE," delights Bobby as if he were on an amusement park ride and not a small plane that could erase both our existences in a literal and figurative flash.

BAM!

A fireball from Zeus detonates in a burst of white heat, rattling the plane, blinking the lights and setting off the seatbelt signs.

My fingers pry into the armrest looking for a safe hold.

"Now that's what we call ball lightning," says Bobby excitedly. "Damn, you're a lucky man. Guy out here could go a decade and never see such a beautiful thing."

I want to answer with a snide remark, but this time fear trumps sarcasm. Besides, if I open my mouth, more than words might fly out.

Darkness envelops the cabin as the clouds swallow us whole. The storm riots on top of us, behind us, under us, everywhere, cloaking the windows in dark gray and shaking the plane as if a toy in a child's hand.

My synapses cross and logic goes out the window. My mind is now convinced that this is it, a life cut short by half.

My body contorts like it touched a hot wire.

Sweat beads on my forehead. My throat swallows uncontrollably.

Something resembling a whimper emanates from a previously undiscovered vocal cord deep in my nasal cavity.

And that's when everything went black.

I'm told we have an internal 'fight-or-flight' mechanism, but what happens when you can do neither? My brain obviously went through that very checklist and just checked out.

I come to after we're safely on the ground. The entire plane has already broken into nervous laughter, everyone comparing this storm to the hundreds of others they'd collectively flown through.

I am apparently fortunate as no one can remember a better storm than this one.

Bobby grasps me on the arm with a giant calloused paw. "Welcome to Lincoln." He hands me a card. "If you ever need anything paved, give me a call. I'll do you right. Go Huskers!"

"Uh, sure thing," I say with a stupid twang I think will make me fit in. I tuck the 'Hogan Paving: We Pave Your Way' card into the shirt pocket I'll never look in again.

I drive through the town of Lincoln and the tension of the flight has faded as fast as the storm clouds. The air smells clean and the sky as open as any I can remember, almost like it rises higher here.

But something's bothering me. They say your life is supposed to flash before your eyes when you think it's about to end. Mine didn't. I couldn't think of anyone to think of at that moment, no one who'd truly and deeply miss me, no one who'd mourn my loss or mark my place in this world. Yeah, they'd say nice things at the funeral, but you always do about dead people.

HONK!

"Sorry lady." The woman in the Grand Prix just shakes her head as I flounder in the intersection I'm not supposed to be in. Some nice guy waves me through.

I ground my mind in reality and take in the sights of this frisky college town.

The city of Lincoln is colored a little like a load of laundry you washed by mistake with a new red shirt. It's hard to find a store or door that hasn't been touched by the color red or one of its faded variants.

As much note as the red colors are the bright smiles and carefree looks on the faces I pass. Almost childlike, it seems this part of the world hasn't grown up with the idea that you have to grit

your teeth and watch your every step to get
through the day.

Don't they realize how hard life is, that bulging
veins and heart palpitations are signs of
accomplishment?

And there in the heart of the country's heartland is
'The Den,' a bustling, bare boned fitness center.

I'm told that Denny is working out in the corner,
and so he is.

Denny is a literal and figurative machine.

Standing six feet plus and muscled far beyond life's
needs, he lifts and runs, pushes and pulls with an
inner passion. It courses through him, the passion,
a wellspring of spirit that infects all around him.

There's no one more intense in the room. There
may be no man more intense anywhere.

All near him move at a faster pace, as if driven by
an unheard cadence.

Just a casual look would tell you that Denny is a
man on a mission. But knowing that mission,
understanding that mission, involves a little work.

Well, not so much, but you have to ask.

He is a man's man with a soul that most would equate with a woman's. Now some would take that to mean weak. Not at all. He's at home in his knowledge of self and speaks from his heart and connects with his eyes in a way that would make most men uncomfortable, but with Denny his self-awareness is a towering strength. No fake male facade here, he doesn't have time for it.

"Doin' legs today," says Denny. "You in?"

"Yeah," I say, feeling the insecurity of a man with toothpicks for legs.

Denny stands up and rips off his sweat bottoms.

I gawk like the mindless soul I am.

Denny does not have legs.

To be more accurate, he has one and a quarter legs, half of one leg and all but a foot of the other.

My stare lingers far too long. He looks at his 'legs' and nods with recognition.

"Car accident. Guard rail cut through the car and left one leg on the dashboard and a foot in the backseat. Politically I lean to the left, but everywhere else I lean to the right," he jokes and begins pounding out leg presses with such intensity I wince.

His legs are half human and half man made. He calls his prosthetics by name, one Viper and the other Nike.

He works me out for what seems like a day of hours; my body is tortured, but I am determined not to go down.

During the workout, we talk and talk and talk.

I learn that Denny's legs aren't his only issue in life.

He also has a disabled son and is battling hepatitis C. God put a lot on his plate for sure. I can't imagine.

I thought, why him? And that's what I ask.

He's quick to respond. "I don't ask why anymore. That question has never led to anything good in my life." I've heard that before.

I learn his motto is 'no excuses, no limits.' While others look for excuses, Denny looks right past them.

"You can choose happiness regardless of what is going on around you," he says with emphasis.

If anyone can make that statement it's Denny, but that doesn't mean I buy it. Then again, how can I look at this man's determined face and think it not true? "I'm not sure I believe that," I challenge.

"How can you choose happiness when everything's going against you?"

He shakes his head as if I don't get it.

"Everyone is going to have tragedy and pain in life. It is how you respond to adversity that determines whether that event will cause positive or negative change in your life."

"But doesn't it get you down?"

"Of course," he smiles. "I'm not numb. I feel the negatives of my situation, but I choose to focus on the positives. To a certain extent, my life didn't start until after I lost my legs. It's been a blessing, because it was then that I realized that everything was my choice. Legs or no legs, I choose!

"Not the car, not the guard rail, not whether or not I have my feet, not the hepatitis. Me. Once you realize that and stop blaming your upbringing, the weather, the stars, whatever, you grow many times your size. Like the Grinch's heart," he smiles.

I probe further, becoming a reporter. "But it can't make you happy to have all of this happen to you."

"I disagree it can make me stronger, wiser and more loving and, therefore, happier. I've learned to appreciate everything in life. I also know that whatever life brings me, good or bad, I'll find a way to grow stronger. I have to. I have a family that needs me. What if my son sees me down all the time? What does that do to him?"

My mind flickers with enlightenment.

"I never thought about the effect my happiness has on others. I always thought my happiness was my business."

He puts an extra fifty pounds on the leg press! I groan. Denny watches me struggle with a half grin.

"Pain is inevitable, suffering is a choice. And to me, choosing unhappiness is self-defeating and selfish. It darkens your world, almost guarantees failure and lessens the quality of life for all around you. Your happiness or unhappiness affects everyone in your life. I may not have much in life compared to others, but I choose to inspire people. I choose to make them better. They look at me and think: 'What excuse do I have?' No excuses, no limits. I turn my negatives into positives."

"You've inspired me," I manage to get out as the weight collapses back on me. I'm done and desperately hoping he is too.

"Thanks. It took me a while to understand that true love involves sacrificing the self-indulgence of unhappiness."

What? I become indignant. "The self-indulgence of unhappiness? Sometimes people can't help it if they're unhappy."

He nods, as if to say he's thought this before. And then he unleashes a line of unbound wisdom that should be marked through time.

"Everyone defines their own criteria for happiness."

Okay, I feel overwhelmed and underwhelmed at the same time, but the complexity defined by his simplicity cannot be overstated.

"Happiness is a choice." His face changes acknowledging his own pain.

"I'm not sure I get it."

"When this first happened to me I was overwhelmed by sadness, by self-pity. But in a way it felt comforting. You can get caught up in the power of sadness, because it makes you feel. Sadness is like a drug, because the feelings are so powerful and all of us want to feel. I mean really feel. Deep. In your bones. In your soul."

He looks up at nothing, remembering.

"I think sadness is deep like that. It was a Tuesday. I don't remember the date, but it was a Tuesday, a Tuesday morning. After so many days that ran together, that one stuck out. I walked into the back yard and my son was on a swing, just rocking back and forth."

Denny looks down, almost like he's looking inside himself.

"He was crying. My son, Denny Jr., was crying.

"I looked at him and asked what was wrong.

"He wouldn't look at me.

"He wouldn't even stop swinging.

"He just said three words.

"Is it me?

"Oh my God.

"Those words.

"His eyes.

"They ripped into me. They ripped me apart.

"I couldn't speak.

"I can't tell you what that did to me. It was like I lost my legs all over again. Worse.

"I felt so selfish, so miserable, so... worthless."

A look of pride takes hold.

"That's when I chose to be happy. You've got to cut it off and say enough's enough. You play the hand you're dealt and you do it with a smile on your face. I realized that I was choosing unhappiness for me and for him."

He takes up his towel mercifully signaling the end of this masochism we call 'good fer ya.' The Viper clomps in uneven cadence marking his walk across the gym, drawing eyes from all around him.

Rather than recoil from their prying stares, surely viewing a sideshow freak, Denny seems to draw strength from them. A strange pride, bordering on arrogance, because he knows he can take life's best shots. Could they?

Denny's personal struggles are his greatest strength. I'd read where Lance Armstrong said the same thing after beating cancer and then winning his ten thousandth Tour de France, but now I'm seeing the power and strength of adversity overcome up close... and it is palpable.

Bending over he takes off Viper, massaging his stump, and I realize his 'arrogance' is really my own insecurity. All he wants is to give people his gift.

He puts an arm around me and gives me that look I would normally call feminine. But now I think maybe it's really a different wavelength of understanding most guys are afraid to experience. I drop my fear and let him in.

"Happiness is not a massive point of no return; it's a life philosophy. If you actively choose happiness every day, it will be yours."

My look tells much.

"Another convert," smiles Denny.

§

Carl laughs. "Makes you feel bad for complaining about the weather, doesn't he?"

"He's all attitude. I think I'm starting to believe."

"So am I," returns Carl, hardly talking about the same thing.

"I mean, believe that happiness is a choice. Everyone I've met has chosen happiness despite their circumstances."

Without a word Carl slides an envelope across the desk with a note. I read the note.

---

### Happiness is a Choice

Your decisions and your outlook, not your condition and environment, determine your happiness in life. You will never be truly happy if you make your happiness dependent on circumstance, because circumstances will always change. - Love 'till time ends, Dad

---

# Secret Nine
## The Forgiver

I open the envelope.

*Serena Tyers*
*High Gate Farms, Sconset*
*Nantucket, MA*

I am eager to complete my journey. The highs, lows, lefts and rights have turned my normally steady brain into a hunk of gray taffy, pulled and stretched, kneaded and turned.

The salt air of this far away (which is what Nantucket means) New England island refreshes my mind even as it takes the edge off my frazzled senses. In fact, the swirling air seems to have taken the edge off everything on the island, like someone came through with a giant pumice stone and buffed everything smooth.

My plodding pregnant horse rides next to, actually behind Serena, and her horse, a deep black stallion named Trooper.

Serena doesn't look like a bitter woman; that's because she's not. Not now anyway.

That doesn't mean she wasn't or doesn't feel it some times.

Burned by life as all of us are at some point, she spent much of her early life upset, mad at the world for things she had no control over.

She had a decent job, she wasn't short on looks or personality, but she was miserable.

It happened that when she was little she came home early from school one day and saw her father with a woman who was not her mother.

Sworn to secrecy, she held it inside, secretly hating herself and her father. When she got older, she told her mother and vowed never to forgive him, to hold him hostage for the terrible things he did.

In so doing she trapped her entire family in hate. Her mother secretly hated her for telling the truth that broke up the marriage. She hated her father for what he did and her mother for what she didn't. He hated himself for obvious reasons.

This was perhaps the most important secret I would learn.

It wasn't a conversation I was looking to have, but I uncorked her bottled emotion by searching for answers to my own guilt and it sprayed out like champagne. Still feels good to talk about it, I guess.

"I was the angriest person you'd ever met. Angry at the world. Angry at myself. Angry at everyone in my life," she tells me as our horses pick though the jagged rocky trail, the Atlantic Ocean crashing nearby.

Trooper seems to lead with one side, stepping past the rocks and sticks and finally out onto the windswept beach dotted with sunbathers and umbrellas. The horses take to the sand with ease.

"I swore I would never forgive them, but I didn't realize I was swearing to a life of unhappiness. It infected all of my relationships and they rotted out from underneath me."

Her thick Boston accent paints her words with drama.

"I turned 30. Then 31. Then 32. I was still alone. I was becoming numb. I started looking at adoption. And it struck me that I would be adopting a child into my hate. I couldn't do it. I had to figure it out."

"I think I know where you're coming from," I offer as encouragement. "How did you figure it out?"

"The horses. That's why I give lessons on the weekends; they symbolize my freedom from myself."

"The horses?" I ask with brows raised.

"I was cleaning out the stalls one day and

everything in the world was getting to me. Well,
Trooper here started acting up. I didn't think at
the time that it was me upsetting the horse. They
can sense it, you know?

"The more Trooper got upset, the more I got upset
at Trooper. I treated him so badly. He reared back
and knocked me over. I turned my head and there
was a rake leaning up against the wall next to me.
It was like all of my demons rushed into my hands.
I picked it up and swung it with a fury I didn't
know I had. It smashed into his head with the
most sickening sound I've ever heard."

A tear runs down her cheek.

"I just lost it."

I look at Trooper. I didn't realize it before, but one
eye is closed, sewn shut with scars.

"I thought about it every day for a month. It was
the worst feeling in the world. I thought about it
and thought about it. He didn't mean it and I
didn't mean it. It just happened and it was awful.
Awful.

"None of us, except the psychopaths of the world,
hurt people because we enjoy it. But we're humans
and we have problems and we don't always know
the best way to deal with them or to make
ourselves feel whole again. Sometimes we do

hurtful things because at the time they seem like the right things. Sometimes it feels like there's no choice.

"It's only later, after the wave of emotion passes, that we can see the dominoes of pain insecurity sends crashing through our lives. I understand that now. And I know that my father is battling his own demons.

"I'm not sure when exactly, but as some point it hit me that I was a prisoner to my own anger and hurting others in the process. In order to escape I had to unlock the door of hate."

"That's a noble thought," I say, "but I'm not willing to forgive certain people. They don't deserve it."

She bends over and strokes Trooper's neck. "That's the mistake I made. Forgiveness not about them; it's about you. If you fail to forgive, you condemn yourself to live in the past. Self-loathing and grudges require enormous energy and drain your life force. If you don't forgive another, you put that person in charge of your time and energy and make them the source of yet more pain."

Now, this makes perfect sense, but I still don't buy it. "How can I forgive someone who wronged me? It goes against all instinct."

We dismount our horses back at the barn,
Trooper's head cocked to keep his eye on Serena,
not a wary eye, a loving one.

"Now, I didn't say forget, I said forgive. No one
wants to be a stooge, but you come to realize that
grudges hurt you more than anyone else. When
you forgive yourself and others, you give yourself
the freedom to start anew and the time and energy
to invest in things that bring true reward."

Her eyes wet.

"I took out a picture of my father one day, the one I
saved in my wallet. Can you believe I kept a
picture of him? Silly, huh?

"I stared at it for I don't know how long. Then I
struck a match and lit the corner. It burned kind
of uneven, like life I guess, until the flame finally
consumed him. All that was left were charred
ashes. I brushed them away and with them... my
hate. I was done. Done with hating and hoping. I
just accepted what was and what is.

"See, I didn't forget, but I did forgive and once I
forgave him and her, something really, I don't
know, magical happened. I forgave myself.
Forgiving them gave me the power to forgive
myself."

I look away pondering the thought. "I think I believe that, but even so it can be tough to remember sometimes."

"Anytime I forget, I look at Trooper. I don't want to hurt either one of us again."

Trooper paws at the ground as if he can understand us.

"Thanks for the lesson."

"It's harder to learn than riding, that's for sure," she pats Trooper on the side with a loving smile.

I swear he winks at me with that good eye.

The waves crash in the distance.

§

"Isn't Sconset beautiful?" Asks Carl.

"Yeah," I say wondering where he's heading.

"Are you in a forgiving mood?"

"I don't know. I guess I have to be."

"We all have to be," he finishes the conversation looking almost Yodaesque.

I'm sad and happy right now, as if there's been some strange transference of power. Without a word Carl slides an envelope across the desk with a note, but this time he does something different. He leans over and shakes my hand. I read the note.

---

### Happiness Requires Forgiveness

To be truly happy, you must forgive yourself and everyone in your life. All humans make mistakes and fail again and again. You must accept your mistakes and those you care about as part of the process of learning. - Love 'till time ends,
Dad

---

# Secret Ten
## The Gift

I open the envelope:

*"Little" Joey*
*Room 107, Children's Hospital*
*Philadelphia, Pennsylvania*

Four weeks to the day my father was laid to rest,
on the order of his will, I meet the last person on
the list.

I ask to see 'Little' Joey, room 107.

"He's in the second door on the left, Mr. Mathews.
It's great to meet you."

How did she know my name?

I open the door and there is Joey.

His tiny chest struggling for breath underneath
and through the ventilator placed over his face.

His body turns for comfort, but he's strapped in,
hooked up and stuck with tubes that protrude out
of his body.

He can't see me or hear me, but I can feel it, he
knows I'm there.

"Joey's going to make it, he's a strong kid. Always
laughing and playing. He is a special, special boy.

We're going to miss him," says the young nurse off to the side. I didn't even notice her.

"I can't tell you how grateful we are for your foundation's donation."

"Donation?" I stumble.

"Yes, that kind of money can do so much. It must feel wonderful to work for such a great organization, Mr. Mathews."

My mind sorts through facts, trying to find the one that will tell me what the heck she's talking about. As I look away to think and I notice the room is wallpapered with 'get well' cards.

"He's got a lot of friends," I admire.

She smiles. "He sure does. People stop by here all the time just to see him. He's got a gift. Anyone who comes in here, no matter how bad they're feeling or what they're battling, leaves smiling. I've never seen anything like it."

"What's wrong with him?" Not sure if I should know or not.

"He has a ventricular septal defect, an opening in the wall separating the atria from the ventricles. It is kind of like having a hole in your boat and constantly having to bail out water. He's only four."

I look at her with slight bewilderment.

"He has a hole in his heart," she qualifies.

My face drops. My stomach pits.

"No, it's okay. The prognosis is good. He'll live a full life. Anyway, I just wanted to thank you personally. My son is also here."

Her face shows unending pain.

"We're not sure he's going to make it, but it gives me and my husband hope to have your support."

"I'm happy to help," I say almost as a question.

Tears and thanks in her eyes, she gives me a hug and walks out of the room.

What the heck?

Obviously, my instinct was right; I have been set up.

But right now all I can think about is this boy and his secret.

I take him in through my eyes.

All the way in.

As deep as deep can go.

And then it hits me.

A giant wave of recognition slamming my reality into the ground, sending my mind off into the currents, slung to the far sides of consciousness.

I can't say it's a surprise. I think I always knew this in a way.

That nose. It's a damn giveaway.

I walk up close and look at Joey's face.

That jutting jaw.

I take in his cheeks.

Then his eyebrows.

I hold his hand.

Years of unexpressed pain condense into tears. I feel lightheaded, dizzy.

A surge of emotion crashes over me, shuttering through every bone, every muscle.

My heart beats faster and faster. The room gets fuzzy.

I feel as if I'm hanging onto the cliff of consciousness.

Right then, Joey murmurs. The sound of his voice snaps me back to reality.

His eyes flash open and close again.

And the clouds part.

Joey.

Joseph.

My son.

I lie my head down next to his.

My mind is fogged with possibilities, swimming to stay afloat. At some point my brain just shuts down and I fall into a trance, numb. Time drifts on unnoticed.

I stare at his face and say a prayer. Not a religious prayer, but my prayer.

I pray for his good health, for his good fortune and for his happiness.

I pray that I can make this right.

I take him in one more time. My son?

MY son.

I love him more than anything, without reservation or thought of self. I love my son with a painful passion. I'm so happy, so grateful.

The moment lingers on and on, the most beautiful moment of my life. Not the way a father dreams of meeting his son, but perfect nonetheless.

And then I feel it.

Her presence washes over me, enveloping the room with the heat of tenderness.

Even before I turn around, I know. My heart throbs with excitement and, just maybe, hope.

I slowly pan around to the face that has haunted my dreams with regret. The one I desperately wanted to see again, yet told myself I hoped I never would.

Her blinding eyes burn a hole through my being, torching my heart.

Her eyes are his eyes.

How could I ever let her go?

Five years of unspoken thought surge between us;
a thread reaching back in time, binding two
broken souls together.

I don't want to ask why.

I don't want to know how.

I just want to be.

I got it.

As much as a man could get it, I got it.

Life has given me another chance, just a chance,
but that's as much as anyone can ask for.

And I realize that the grand scheme of my father is
the ultimate gift, the lessons that will allow his son
to love. Without his lessons all this would be lost,
tossed on the sad pile of life's missed moments.

But it wasn't.

How could he have known her?

Why didn't she tell me?

A million questions, but the answers don't matter.

The only thing that matters is what's right in front of me.

Right here. Right now. In the moment.

It is all the explanation I need. I now know that asking why is a loser's game.

I give thanks for everything in my life, to my father and the secrets that have given me this moment I will never forget.

I might have been bitter, but I learned to forgive.

I might have hesitated, but I learned to commit.

I might have feared, but I learned to act.

I might have retreated, but learned to embrace change.

I might have seen pain, but now I saw only love.

I might have waited, but I learned happiness does not wait.

I might have wanted more, but I learned the magic of simplicity.

I might have held back, but I learned you get what you give.

Most of all I learned to see the good in everything, accept life's gift, choose happiness on my terms and sacrifice my old indulgences to get it.

No, it wasn't perfect. There were no guarantees anything would work out, but it was perfect imperfection.

A note tacked on the wall catches my attention.

I read the note.

§

### Happiness is a Gift

True happiness is found in giving. Your happiness will give the gift to others in your life and begin the cycle that will return to you. Giving love allows you to step off the roller coaster of highs and lows and puts your mind in a balanced state of happiness. You must love to be loved. Give your love often and with abandon. Choose, give, love, live, forgive, commit, act, think, be... happy!
- Love 'till time ends, Grandpa

# The Epilogue

I stare at my reflection. A changed man looks back with open eyes that are full of life.

I weigh the envelope in my hand as a child would a Christmas present to guess its contents.

I've just returned from my final meeting with Carl. I had so many questions for him. So many things I didn't get. So many things I wanted to know, but he wouldn't answer them. He simply told me that real lessons are lived and I had more to learn. Then, without another word, he slid this envelope across the desk to me.

On the front of it are the words: *the ten signs*

The ten signs of what!? I open the envelope.